# Ask Anything,
# and Your Body Will Answer

# Ask Anything, and Your Body Will Answer:

## *A Personal Journey Through Integrated Awareness*®

by
### Julie J. Nichols, Ph.D.
and
### Lansing Barrett Gresham

NoneTooSoon Publishing
©2000

ISBN 1-893969-00-2


Cover design by Brad Eigen.
Cover image ©2000 PhotoDisc, Inc.

# Acknowledgments

To teachers whose work has been highly influential, including but not limited to June d'Estelle, Moshe Feldenkrais, John Upledger, Jean-Pierre Barral, and Werner Heisenberg, and Gene England, Elouise Bell, both Dorothys, Jeraldene Lovell, Marilyn Graham, and especially Clyde and Carol Juchau;

to editor Dawn Anderson and designers Steve Vistaunet and Brad Eigen;

to supportive family and friends, in-laws and exes, students, colleagues, allies, and guests (you know who you are);

to Barbara Jean;

and to Nick, Big J, Elder Ike in Nagoya, Jessie Liz, and Jacob:

toasts
hugs
and gratitude way beyond words.

JJN Salt Lake City UT
LBG Cotati CA
*July 1999*

*"The ultimate purpose of life—*

*each life, any life, your life this time*

*—is to experience such profound and unconditional gratitude*

*for this life*

*that you would be loath*

*to change any of your many lives' experiences*

*lest that change lead on to a path*

*in which such divine and fulfilling gratitude*

*was not yet present."*

Lansing Barrett Gresham

"Healing is acceptance
embodied in the present moment
and space,
accomplished when there is no longer
resistance in the self
to the current condition—
physically,
capable of doing what you want
without fear of pain
or recurrence;
emotionally
responsive to present moments, instead
of re-creating past hurts;
mentally quiet;
energetically intensely spontaneously
available to interact;
spiritually, unconditionally accepting."

# Authors' Note

For readers familiar with Integrated Awareness® already, this book is a way to review and remember certain historical models and phases of development it has passed through. For those who aren't yet familiar with IA classes, sessions, or teachers, the book may serve as a foundation and inspiration for current work. For both, it's a prelude to the forthcoming *Body's Map of Consciousness*.

On the right side of the page spread you'll find a coherent personal narrative of a composite Touchstone experience. Readers who are more concerned with what IA is about than with character history may want to skip to page 1, leaving the "Introduction" section for later.

On the left side of the page spread are transcriptions of notes of one student's perceptions and interpretations of Lansing Barrett Gresham's words. These are not direct verbatim quotes. They are declarations, aphorisms, and metaphorical explanations, like hundreds spoken, demonstrated, and taught experientially in myriad different ways at Touchstone workshops. In many instances they're composites of statements made several times over the course of several workshops. Generally we've placed them where they're most pertinent to the narrative on the right side of the spread rather than in any other order. All are used with Lansing's permission.

"The feeling of being trapped
between two
seemingly
exclusive
choices
grows from the underlying sense
that neither one is really a choice—
that instead
two equally unsatisfying coercives
are at work:
I have to but I can't,
I want to but I shouldn't,
I need to but others will disapprove.
When a resolution is finally embraced,
it will be comprised of a
mutually
higher
harmonic,
a third choice,
larger than either,
retaining all the essential ingredients
of both."

# INTRODUCTION

**We're evolving a model that can never be finished, because it is carried on the ever-expanding wavefront of human awareness. What we're developing is not a replicable thing. It is contagiously inspirational.**

I grew up in the sixties in a well-to-do conservative household just over the hill from the University of California at Berkeley, that hotbed of liberality and free thought, riot and insurrection. It's a measure of my shelteredness that I knew something was going on on the other side of El Toyonal, but I didn't know exactly what. It didn't impinge much on our orderly life at home.

At school, however, my teachers and friends were agnostic artists, freethinking hippies, writers and seekers. My dad wasn't always pleased with my friendships and enthusiasms, but he subscribed firmly to the principle of free agency, the idea that the greatest gift of earth life is the individual's power to choose, that "all truth is independent in its own sphere."

By the time I graduated from high school in 1971, I rode uneasily a revolving door between two selves: the good girl who knew all the right words, all the right vocabulary (both of language and of action) for pleasing God, my parents, and the conservative leaders of our church, and someone else, secret rebel, idolizer of my friends, indifferent to authority or scripture except insofar as the words sounded beautiful to me.

I wasn't thrilled with the idea of packing off to Utah to go to college. Berkeley sounded better. But I was awarded a full academic scholarship in the land of my grandparents, and Dad threatened

"A miracle:
anything
much greater than you
ever believed
possible."


"Whenever you feel that you MUST
do something
you want,
you cease to enjoy it.
It was, after all, the element of
free will
which gave the spice.
Choice is a function of desire:
you rob the one, you rob the other.
Soul WANTS that you have *embodied choice*."

not to support me if I went anywhere else. I nurtured a secret rebelliousness, on the outside obeying all the rules and making all the grades, but on the inside, growing to hate all that, missing my other life fiercely.

In 1975, while I filled an editing internship in Salt Lake City, I attended a University of Utah religion class whose enlightened teacher suggested that anything Jesus did, all humans can do—all those miracles, all that healing, all that love. I adored the idea. Why *wouldn't* we be able to do those things? Why *wouldn't* they be a built-in part of human experience? I wanted to know the practicalities. *How do we do it?* In my experience, the technicalities weren't being taught anywhere. The concepts, yes. The how-to: no.

Two years later I married, and by 1983 I had three children under six, an unemployed husband, two postsecondary degrees and a part-time (read "dead-end") university teaching job. I knew that a good girl shouldn't feel angry or trapped, but I did. A good girl doesn't quit, she sees things through; she doesn't let anybody know she needs a break. She just works harder, sets her jaw. Tenses her back muscles for the hard labor of pushing through.

But in secret flights of imagination, as I pushed my children on swings in the park, or read them stories, or closed my ears against them while I finished my thesis and began a teaching career, I summoned up visions of a different city, a different environment, a different life—and a certainty that I couldn't have them. I wasn't supposed to.

In 1983 a series of events cascaded into my life at which I still look back with wonder. A friend who had known me in high

"If you don't know
what's 'supposed to be,'
then everything's a discovery
inspiring you to do more.
To learn is to go ahead and explore.
In this world, learning
and healing
are The Same Thing."

"If you don't predict or expect your experience,
then you can have it. "

school visited me, rode around town for a few days with me, saw what I had created for myself in that life. She asked me a few questions and listened to me vent. "Things are fine," I said at one point—another brilliant concession to good-girl appearances. "I just have a few questions."

My wise friend, far from oblivious, said, "You already have your answers, Julie—you just have to find them." The generous implications of these few words unsettled me. They gave me permission to trust my frustration, to let it lead me where I needed to go.

I searched for answers, then, whatever and wherever they were. I dragged my three small children with me to libraries and bookstores, unsure what key words to search for. Because it was acceptable in my world to call this kind of angst a spiritual need (not a mental aberration or an emotional illness), I let that Jesus question drive me—"how did Jesus do what he did, and how can I learn to do it too?" Something about the humaneness of the New Testament Jesus, his good sense, his refusal to pay heed to convention began to appeal as a pattern. I looked at books about the Grail, about myth, about quests. I read Susan Cooper's *The Dark Is Rising* series, a set of novels in which modern children worked with Merlin to drive back the ancient Dark. I found Robert Graves's *The White Goddess,* that dense study of the Celtic origins and female nature of creativity—and it stood directly next to a book whose spine said *Womanspirit Rising: A Reader in Feminist Theology.* I inhaled what was in them both, and passed into my "feminist spirituality" phase. All these synchronicities, all these connections—maybe they were a message about things working in

"A coincidence is a relationship
you don't recognize."

"Consciousness:
the experience of Source
within four dimensions.

Energy:
the means
created by Consciousness
to experience itself."

my behalf if I organized myself to let them. Maybe the universe wasn't my foe after all.

I found intuition classes in Salt Lake and read books on centering and meditation and auric bodies. It was useful to me to consider that intangible faith might be a combination of consciousness and energy, a reality that could be measured, quantified, even photographed. It was useful to me to reframe other concepts too, to recognize that when I manipulated energy from a position of awareness—of conscious choice—I was "creating my own reality," which is a neopagan, feminist-spirituality equivalent to my church's "working out your own salvation." The new physics had proofs that energy is real, that every molecule has consciousness, that my intelligence is not separate from the intelligence of every cell on earth.

I experimented. Our daughter cried incessantly the first six months of her life. One sleepless midnight when I'd had enough of her wakefulness, I held her close and quietly instructed her in word and in energy-bytes through my hands to sleep six more hours. She didn't make another peep, this baby who was usually wakeful all night, until exactly five fifty-nine.

I wrote affirmations and carried them around in my wallet and watched them fulfill themselves. I practiced "abundance thinking" and took conscious responsibility for my health, exercising zealously and having my third and fourth babies at home under the care of midwives who worked with herbs and whole foods.

"When the soul supervises conception,

creating a viable first cell,

it selects

from the many possible genetic combinations available

those ingredients which will make it more likely

for the self to be attracted to experiences,

and capable of engaging in behaviors,

which will lead to a perspective

from which all the experiences of your life

are recognized

as having been necessary.

If you look back

and all the experiences of your life are

necessary,

when you look forward

you're facing your life purpose."

Yet even as I maintained an image of reserved dependability, taught the women's auxiliary in my church congregation, and raised a healthy and bright young family with my husband, in relative solitude—in hiding—I explored feminist theology, "psychic awareness," personal growth, the relationship between consciousness and reality. I kept my findings to myself. I also judged my neighbors, colleagues, and husband for not knowing or seeking what I knew and sought. The rift between my outer life and my inner one grew huge and dangerous.

There was one area of my life where I found a way not to feel split, not to need to hide: the teaching of creative writing. I threw myself into that task, feeling a profound sense of accomplishment when student after student saw their lives validated in writing, and their writing validated by each other and me. I loved counseling with them—it seemed natural, easy, to intuit what their meaning was even when their words were awkward or unclear, and equally easy and intuitive to guide them toward revision and clarity.

And of course I wrote, myself. I wrote about the frustration of trying to be a good mother to three small children. I wrote that I felt terrible about how I reacted when my five-year-old's bicycle was stolen, screamed at him, blamed him. I wrote about my emergency appendectomy, a surprise rush to the hospital after a day of particular obstacles—my reaction to which, I was certain, was the literal root cause of the exploded appendix. Colleagues urged me to submit my essays to journals, to publish, to enter contests—which I sometimes won.

"Most of us would rather not feel
the pain of others.
We actively avoid it
and regularly find ways
to decrease our awareness of the places in ourselves
that resonate with the disharmony
in another.
By choosing to more fully occupy his or her physical being
and increasing his or her willingness to feel the world of another
the IA teacher becomes more vulnerable.
And it is this state of vulnerability–
of increased presence and occupancy on the part of the toucher–
that creates the energetic environment
in which a guest
may feel supported enough to take a new step,
accept a previously hidden truth,
or to forgive at last.
The very process
of greeting another's pain with presence
rather than abandoning either one's self or the other
facilitates the change."
(Marilyn Graham, master's thesis)

I earned a Ph.D., taught classes in "Writing as Healing Practice" at the university and in the community, and taught introductory creative writing to hundreds of young people. I also wrote fiction about people who used energy consciously and explored alternative realities. Some of the stories won prizes. Several saw publication.

But there was still dissatisfaction. I knew I'd made all the decisions to bring me this far, but still, my extracurricular interests fed me more than my daily life, and I didn't know how to stop hiding my secret interests, or how to change the trajectory of my split life. I studied Voice Dialogue, a consciousness modality developed by Hal and Sidra Stone in which energy states can be an avenue to transformation through an increased sense of choice. At the same time, through bodywork, I experienced how the physical body reflects and influences these energy states, as well as how both the physical and the energetic bodies carry imprints of past choices, and are organized to accommodate new choices at any moment.

At an innovative massage school I learned the basics of Swedish massage and shiatsu, shamanism and Western energy healing. In June, 1996, Marilyn Graham, a quiet-voiced, small-boned woman from Petaluma, California, came to the school to teach a set of skills I felt immediately drawn to—expanded states of consciousness, particular qualities of touch, intuitive contacting of all levels of consciousness through the body's structure and energy. When I asked for more information, she directed me to Touchstone, the healing center where she'd received her training.

"If you don't know what's 'supposed to be,'
then everything's a discovery
inspiring you to sense what is.
To learn is to go ahead and explore.
In this world, learning  and healing are the same thing
whenever Right and Wrong
are deleted from your beliefs."

"Fear is excitement without the breathing."

# Show up: it's your best healing tool.

*Cotati, California. 2:00 pm August 3, 1996.*

I'm late. I left Salt Lake City this morning at ten Utah time,
thinking that plane flights and rental cars would move me
smoothly from home to here in plenty of time, but I've never been
to Cotati before and though I was given excellent directions from
the Oakland airport, I'm an hour late for this workshop that started at one, and I'm nervous.

Not just because I'm late, either. This is a Touchstone workshop called "Professional Techniques." Sounds good for telling
my friends at the university; we're always being encouraged to
increase professionalism. What my English Department colleagues don't know is that this course has nothing to do with
teaching writing or literature. Everyone in this class at Touchstone
has trained for months or years in healing processes collectively
called Integrated Awareness⁕, which I was introduced to only a
few weeks ago by a guest instructor at the massage school I attend
part-time in Salt Lake City. The flyer for this Professional
Techniques course describes it *"for those in professional training
only; others by instructor's permission."* There they are, those italics.

The fact is, I'm not "in professional training"—not this kind
of training, anyway. I'm a teacher of writing at a university where
silence is my best strategy for continued employment. I'm a writer
without a book, a hobbyist healer with training but no license, a
frustrated mother of four in a marriage I too often let carry the
blame for whatever I don't like about myself.

"Change your internal rules,
being willing to not
know what will
happen once
you do.
If you cease
wounding yourself,
your system heals."

Dissatisfied with nearly everything, I'm all unspoken desires, unrealized potentials. I've heard words of counsel from conventional and alternative therapists, experienced help from bodyworkers, tried everything from herbs to Oriental body therapy, from Reiki to running. All of them have brought me closer to here, and for that I'm grateful.

I still run. Marathons. They keep me sane. I'm small and lean and strong and I have long red hair, and there are things about my life I dare anyone to tell me I should do differently. Who's a better teacher of creative writing? a better mom? A better juggler, really, of myriad tasks and eclectic interests?

But there are things I'd really like to know how to change. People say, "you're just Type A, you'll never get over it," but I wish it were that simple. I'm tired of being frustrated, weary of seeing my life as a trap. Underneath the anger, my heart hurts. I want something to be different.

I've been told Touchstone is a place where people go who haven't found relief elsewhere, a place to heal once and for all. And I'm nervous. What if it's actually true?

What if it isn't?

With butterflies in my stomach, I walk through the first floor of the classroom building at Touchstone. I don't know where to go once I'm inside. It's a light green, two-story building with many windows on a spacious lot, clean-looking and inviting, plants familiar from my childhood in the Bay Area in boxes around the patio. But I find nothing that looks like a classroom. There are doors, but they all have other names on them than "Touchstone"

"Discipline is good
for performance.
Comfort is good
for learning."

or "Professional Techniques," and the ones that have windows seem to be small offices.

From upstairs, however, I hear laughter. There on the wide staircase are fifty pairs of shoes, set against the wall in a wild array of summer footgear. I slide off my own sandals and pad up the stairs to the glass door at the landing, where I wait a second before I open the door. What's being taught on the other side might change everything.

Through the glass, I can see a crowd of men and women clustered around a massage table in the middle of a skylit room. They lean toward a curly-haired man who sits forward on a stool, his elbows on the table and his hands waving as he talks. I can't hear what he's saying, but I can see that everyone listens intently and there are further rustles of laughter—a good feeling. It looks comfortable. I let myself in, close the door quietly behind me, and sit on the nearest sit-down thing, a stool, back away from the crowd, not wanting to interrupt, hoping they won't notice me yet.

Is the man talking Lansing Barrett Gresham? Probably not. I've been told the founder of Touchstone and creator of Integrated Awareness is in his fifties, "charismatic," "an awesome healer." This man looks too young. I figure he's an assistant, trained by Lansing and sent in to lay groundwork in the mornings. I like his manner. If this is how Lansing teaches his assistant, I'm in the right place. I like what I hear. He talks quickly, concisely, in abstractions and metaphors whose content I don't fully grasp but which feel familiar to me, resonant somehow.

"Every complaint
you have would diminish
in the presence of more
heart."

"I'm relentless.
I tell the truth.
And it helps to love a lot..."

"All healings depend on your state of consciousness," he says. "Fear will keep you out of a state which can facilitate healing; coercion will keep everyone else out. Presence and willingness are the two requirements for healing. Find out what's needed for the guest to be present and willing."

Well, yes, I think, inching a bit closer. This makes sense. It's what I came here for: Integrated Awareness, I've been told, takes for granted that human consciousness is the fundamental tool, increased awareness of choice the foundation of all healing, including the healing of physical disease. I want to hear more.

I determine to stay in the background, to learn through observing, not to say anything yet. Just take it all in, surreptitious. Silence as strategy. Get all I can without exposing myself. That's how I do things, after all.

And the personable young teacher, finished with his unit of thought, turns straight to me. "You must be Julie," he says, coming across the room to take my hand. I'm suddenly shy. "I'm Julie," I agree, and he says, "I'm Lansing." *But nobody told me you were handsome, I think and don't say. I thought you would be big, in body and in ego, and I thought you would have white hair.* So much for expectations: he is none of these things. Instead he reaches out to me with his heart—I can feel it—and he feels young, spilling warmth, affection, invitation. I feel strangely vulnerable. I want to tell him *shhhhh, just let me sit quiet and be invisible.* I will learn soon enough that invisible isn't Lansing's style, and that of course he knows how new I am to this—he's fully aware that I haven't had all the experiences his other trainees have. But he's invested time and energy and permission in the idea that I belong here

"Source gives rise to Self,
Self to Consciousness,
Consciousness to energy,
energy to pattern and form,
both of which always
move and change."

anyway. He leads me back to the table in the center of the room.

"This is Julie," he tells the group, still holding my hand unaffectedly, kindly. "She's probably—no, she is—the only person here who hasn't had a class or a workshop in this classroom before. So help her. Look out for her. Make her feel welcome. She's come all the way from Utah." Murmurs of appreciation, kind and curious looks. And then we get to work.

Sitting scattered on stools around the classroom, where maybe a dozen tables are set up, we listen to Lansing as he walks among us. I'm struck by the ease of his posture, the natural grace of his walk. "Everything is energy and consciousness," he says. "Your body is a composite of the way you create the world to be. The movements of your structure reveal the quality and dynamic of your energy, and your energies are even closer approximations to your composite consciousness."

I pay close attention, not just to his words, which, except for the words "energy" and "consciousness," sound like a foreign language; but also to the feeling in the room, the sea of something fine we're swimming in. I'm a teacher, from a long line of teachers and pragmatists. It's my habit to convert what I hear to something I can teach, so that I'm always weighing the manner of presentation, evaluating the beauty and utility of the thing taught. I've been involved for years now in ongoing training from many enlightened teachers. Interested in the craft, I watch teachers a lot. And I find I'm drawn to what's happening in this room. It feels good—active, enlivening, intelligent—despite the initial unfamiliarity of the phrases I'm hearing. They're dense, poetic, sometimes almost opaque. I'm compelled to listen carefully.

"Congruence:

occupying the same space

at the same time.

The more aspects of you that are congruent

the more authentic

you feel, and the more exalted

your choices."

*Willingness to change, and timing,*
*can be cued by*
*congruence of energetic body and structure.*

*Healing is never about "getting rid of"*
*—it's about adding new choices.*

*Vulnerability*
*is being present AND available for connection.*

I like these. I like their pithiness, how much they require me to be aware of, how much I sense is behind them: there's plenty more to harvest from these than from the usual "tips for better healing." It's going to take some time to take in their full implications.

But even more than the richness of their implications, I like how I'm being taught. No: shown. Modeled. Something about the way Lansing walks among us, talking from the top of his head and a depth of heart, demonstrating easily, moving from one mood and mode to another to show us what he means. It's not just about wise aphorisms. It's about tuning, like lining us up with the pitch of a certain level of meaning, a nonverbal synchronization that more than compensates for the muddling the words sometimes induce in those of us new to this.

I'm drawn to these new words, words about "levels of consciousness" and the relation between the physical structure and nonphysical reality. They're a little startling in their implications, and being so startled—so "beneficently confused"—relieves, for a

"We want to move
out of resistance
into confusion and then
on toward discovery and integration.
Inducing confusion
to alleviate blockages
is beneficent confusion
-deliberately creating minor chaos in the body
to allow opening to new choices.
We work with our physical structure to revise beliefs.
It's a highly refined vehicle, this body,
divinely organized and conceived.
We can let it do infinitely more
than we have.  It's built to change
-to be dynamic, constantly in flux, adaptable,
responsive to choice.
Everything on the planet supports
the pervasiveness, the brilliance, the lessons of choice.
We adapt by cutting off choice.
In this sphere of existence,
more fundamental than gravity (which is a form of intelligence)
is movement.
When we make a rule, when we cut off choice,
it shows up in the body as movement
stopped.
All other parts of the body rearrange themselves
to adapt to these immobilities.
Restoring mobility restores choice."

moment, the irritation I carry so much of the time, the constant undercurrent like an itch and an illness turning all joys brown.

I make poems because symbols and analogies make richer sense to me than bald facts. It's easy, familiar, affirming, to accept the idea that structural glitches, difficulties in the body, reflect difficulties in nonphysical aspects of my life, choices refused, possibilities cut off. But it's not just a concept. Lansing presents us with a floor process that shows it's as real as my bones and blood.

We clear the floor, spread out on our backs. To begin with, Lansing suggests a posture, a way to organize our physical bodies to reveal how patterns of thinking or feeling or believing manifest themselves in our structure. I lie face up on the floor, alert and focused inward. "Place one arm palm down and by your side," we're prompted, "the other palm up with elbow bent so that the hand is above the head. Focus on the physical body. Move the hand above the head as far as possible before encountering resistance, focusing fully on the muscles and connective tissue and bone and blood of your hand. You may be able to move only a sixteenth of an inch before you hit a glitch. Don't rush this. Move slowly and carefully, and note where your muscles stop."

Yes: my muscles move my hand barely a sixteenth of an inch before it stops. And then another sixteenth, and another. There's no easy sailing here. Speed bumps all over the place. But that's all there is to that instruction: just note how far the physical body moves before it halts. Another time we might explore the content of the blockage. But this time, all we do is observe. And wonder: am I so harnessed, then—does my body really hold all these knots? Are these all *nots* my head prescribes?

"Every human is comprised
of many levels of consciousness
(LOCs)
—fso many that science
will be occupied for a long time
finding the rhythms
and evidences of all of them.

*The physical body:*
dense as bone,
the one through which all others are accessed,
always in the here and now.

*The emotional body:*
a field coherent
as energy or structure,
connects all of us
as sheets of connective tissue
bind all body parts.
Emotion motivates us to action,
tends to fixate in the past.

*The mental body:*
our most familiar field
interfaces with the nervous system,
is distorted by "right" and "wrong"
clarified by inclusivity
designed to tell us when
truth
is greater
than our personal beliefs."

"Now," comes the next instruction, "focus on the energetic body. This time, reach as far as possible energetically, without leaving your body. Don't move your physical body at all. Again, note where the first barrier is. How far can you reach energetically without hitting a barrier?"

Well, I ought to be able to do this; I've worked with energy before, moved my energy around without moving my physical body. I imagine surely that I should be able to go clear to the ends of the universe if I intend it. Surely the energetic body has no barriers. But my energy gets only about halfway to the ceiling. I'm surprised, both by the short distance and by the independence of the response. I didn't think it would happen this way, and I can't muscle that energy into moving some strong-willed distance. My energetic body just goes as far as it goes. It must know some things I don't, about what I believe I can and cannot do. I'm a little frightened by it.

Next we're told, "Focus on the emotional body. Reach, with the overhead hand, for 'the last thing.' It can be any 'last thing'— the last candy bar, the last redwood tree, the last kind embrace. But it's the last, and you want it desperately. Again, note where the barriers are."

This one gets tears out of me, because I can't do it. I lead from my heart, pouring myself toward "the last thing," but my hand won't go there. It just doesn't move. What is this? Some big rule, some self-imposed restriction against having what I want, a denial of desires that's been seeping into my daily life for years now? Surely I never intended it to get so out of hand that I can't even move toward what I want!

*"The energetic body:*
*a broad vibrational band,*
localized expressions of which include auras and chakras,
is involved in alltime, allspace,
perceptible as fluid or light around us,
predisposes the shape of the physical structure,
foretells disease ,
indicates physical health.
*The spiritual or karmic body:*
links in an instant,
like the synapses of nerves,
to times and places
even lifetimes
beyond the here and now."

"If you can't make a movement, behaviors are denied you
and therefore experiences also.
Therefore, you are not connected.
What you can't move is dead to you."

"What rule stops
the movement? We immobilize
—prevent choice—
by rules
and
judgment."

I feel sad. It's familiar, surfacing from careful burial beneath the anger, the sense of entrapment, which I've come here to correct. It's a little scary, a little too visible. There's an inkling that something essential might actually shift if I let myself examine what this piece of information reveals.

"Now focus on the 'karmic' body, or another way to say it is to focus on your life purpose. You don't even need to know what it is. Something in your body knows. Just intend for your life purpose to be the force behind the movement, and reach with the overhead hand for the thing without which your life would be nothing. Reach till you find a barrier, and note what happens."

My hand reaches further with this one than it did when my heart led, but it still stops before I get anywhere near "the thing without which my life would be nothing." What is *that*? Teaching? Writing? My children? But none of these feels like the entirety. I'm teetering on the edge of something. What if I go there and can't name it? I do as Lansing says, give over to intention, reach. And my hand stops halfway there. Wherever "there" is.

Now we're told to combine any two of the movements we've just explored. "Add the energetic body to your physical effort to reach as far as you can, and see what happens to the barriers," is the instruction; "or add the 'karmic' body to the emotional body's effort to reach for that 'last thing.'"

Mildly confused, surrendering to the words, I add my energetic body to the emotional body's heart-led effort to reach for the "last thing." This is interesting: my hand moves quite a bit further than it did without the energetic body's help, maybe three or four inches. Hey. Look, this is easy. I feel quickened, more alive.

"Recruit all parts of you
to restore mobility. Discover where
the points of most effort are.
Go to them
with intent to be
curious
about who or what.
Focus on them.
What's interesting
is noting position
and degree of effort and tension
and allowing it to change.
It's all information."

I want to stay in this place of possibility. But I'm not going to tell anybody yet, in case it isn't real.

"Now try other combinations. Note which combinations help you most. Note which bodies you can recruit to greatest effect."

I play around with this. Adding my energy also helps the physical effort, but not the "life purpose" quite as much. Ah: when I add my heart to the "life purpose" aim, all of me feels propelled, electrified. It's cool.

Then there's one last word. "Now, with your palm-down hand and arm, press down NO. As you do this, go for what you want with whichever of your bodies you wish. Watch what happens."

When I press down "no," no matter what "body" I set out to use, I curl up in a tight ball, contracted and hard. Nothing lets me go. Everything feels strangled, from my inside center outward. It's icky. I use that word later, during discussion, to describe how it feels. To feel so switched on for a moment, and then so shut down—maybe this isn't all just good feely stuff.

Everyone else leaves the classroom for a break. I lie curled up on the floor, replaying in my body first that rush of freed-up vitality, and then the unmistakable "no." I just want to be with it for a little, because it feels so central—not in my heart exactly, more like inside its beating; not in my lungs, but in the waveform of my breath. I want to know what this is.

When I ask Lansing, he says, shrugging, as if everyone should know, "You hit a rule." It puzzles me. *What* rule? I want to know more about it. But he turns away, and somebody says, grinning at my puzzlement, "What rule doesn't matter as much as that you figure out what to recruit to get past the block."

*"Table sessions:*

we are all

always connected.

The guest determines

the subject and extent of change,

making a wish or contract or declaration...

trained teachers then

jointly, through energetics

and hands-on support,

facilitate changes in all LOC's

such that blockages

and resistances

can be turned to allies and

the wish or contract fulfilled.

Combined helpers' energies,

their

presence and willingness

increase exponentially the possibility

of change for the

person on the table.

Table sessions honor

the power of community,

of connected focus."

Oh, is that all?

Lansing asks me if I'd like to serve as the subject of a demonstration, a table session around the topic of reorganizing life meaning. It sounds like a pretty ambitious task. But why not? I say sure. I'd love it.

When everyone has gathered again in the classroom after the break, I sit on a table, and Lansing and I talk. It takes some time to "come to contract." Lansing asks me to name the dominant rule I follow in my interactions with people. I tell him the rule is "Come off smart. Be good." I could just as well say, "Hide," or "Be right." They're all the same thing, they're all (I get the idea as I talk with him) rules that help create the constant anger, the inability to relax, the ardent loneliness and sense of separation.

He asks, "Who would you disappoint if you didn't 'come off smart'? If you weren't right?"

I say (an easy, glib answer), "The Committee of Men." He doesn't even blink. He says, "Oh yeah. Dad. Church. God. Understood."

He takes my hand, again with that kindness, that focused attention. More than clinical skill, it's a palpable comforting that reaches into me, includes all of me, even the anger. It diffuses my usual defensiveness.

"How could you restate your perception about your place on earth so that it's no longer a source of anger, but instead inspires

"We all have survival wiring for all choices.
All of us can make all choices.
But even though we have that,
if we're not willing
to make the choices
or take the consequences,
we stiffen or contract.
But when we
connect—when we choose to
belong—we expand.
Practically every form of healing
involves
expanding in the face of unpleasantness."


"To be vulnerable means
to be present and available for connection."



"Every component of the physical structure
has vibrational intrinsics
corresponding to certain
aspects of human emotional
reality.
Everywhere you go in yourself,
aspects of yourself are pre-set
to a harmonic
of that place. "

you and frees you to be yourself?" Lansing asks. "Let me suggest that you go for big."

"Big"?

His questioning is gentle. I'm struck by the range of tools in use: IA doesn't seem to be merely uncommon knowledge about the body, or a matter, either, of psychological expertise. Both, clearly, are in the hands of a skilled healer. But they're not all. The catalytic ingredient is personal. Later I learn to call it "presence," the property of "showing up," and "vulnerability," which includes conscious connectedness; but just now it feels like kindness, courteous and complete attentiveness, and I'm not about to turn it down.

I make an attempt at the restatement I've been asked to frame. It takes a minute. The opposite of my rule is something like, "I don't have to be right. I'm okay as is. I am—I'm already everything I came here to be." I say something like that, with a question in my voice. I feel like a child.

There is applause. Someone in the crowd calls, "You go, girl!" I have the feeling all these watching people are delighted for me to choose a big change, because it will affect them too. Each person's healing relieves us all.

Lansing has me lie on the table, cups my head in his hands. He recruits from the class several assistants who, with intent to serve my healing, place hands on body sites that carry the same vibration and frequency as the thing I declared to be my obstacle, that insistence on being right so as not to be rejected. Lansing directs those working with him to tune to my consciousness in such a way that I can experience a revision of my agreement with my father and mother about my life, my conception and birth.

"Our two sides are organized asymmetrically.

In your body's map of consciousness,

the structure of the left side corresponds

to the way you embody femaleness, the

way you react to the female gender.

The structure of the right side corresponds

to the way you embody maleness, the

way you react to the male gender.

What is more medial

is more related to the core of you;

what is more lateral has to do

with 'other,' what is not you.

To the front

is more related to the personality

and to this body and this lifetime;

more to the back

is more unconscious,

not so much this body or this life.

In the body as a whole and

in each organ, what is closer to

earth is older,

what is higher is younger,

since lessons tend to accumulate

with gravity."

I listen carefully, my eyes closed, attending to the variety of sensations my body experiences through my helpers' hands. He sends someone to my right ring finger, another to my spleen; someone else places one hand on top of my left shoulder and another underneath it. After a while I give up trying to attend to them all. The whole effect is pleasantly confusing, rich, beyond my current capacities to make sense of it. All I can do is relax and go along.

Lansing pauses to instruct. "I'm a relentless observer," he tells the class. "I assume the universe is not my enemy, and I assume I'm not maladapted. Anyone can observe what I observe. Anybody can do what I'm doing."

I'm not so sure. There's the comfort of technique, transmissible discrete skills students come here to learn and practice; but there's also the mystery of gift, and the honing of that gift, and the commitment to service without which any gift has less effect, and which I'm sure I do not have right now, may never have, to the degree I sense it here.

All hands tune to take me back to prenatal moments and birth. The intention is to lend that time a quality of joy and expectation I haven't up to now acknowledged. Part of me wants to laugh—hold it, isn't it a little late for that?—but everyone's taking it pretty seriously, so I keep my eyes shut and pay attention. I seem to be moving backward in time—getting smaller. Certainly I don't feel like an articulate, independent adult any more.

At a point which we all seem to know is "birth," I hang over the edge of the table for a long time, just as I hung out in the womb, three weeks overdue. I appreciate Lansing's instructions to

"Specific areas of the body
resonate
with the vibrations
of certain states
intrinsic
to the
earth: shame, sadness,
betrayal,
gratitude,
joy."

"Taking note of structural patterns
gives insight into the rules we allow
to run our lives.
Changing structure will change
underlying energy,
and vice versa.   As we invite
alternative future outcomes, our bodies respond
differently."

his student helpers that I be assisted toward an "elegant" conclusion, since I'm being supported in midair in a gawky, awkward position, surely uncomfortable for Lansing's assistants who are bearing my weight, and for Lansing himself, who holds my head and shoulders, waiting, letting me wait. Nothing in me wants to move, as I float right there. I'm not thinking, not planning; I seem to be an observer watching this unknown woman arch herself off the table and relive her natal fits and starts, deciding something, waiting for some internal signal to carry on. It lasts an amazingly long time from where I am, eyes closed, far away inside myself.

Suddenly my body simply begins to move again. All those pairs of hands direct me gracefully back onto the table, back into the classroom, back into present time, to rest.

I lie still, taking note of the very real shifts I feel, a collection of tingles and stillnesses, newly smooth places and newly stirred. Lansing directs the other students to carry out similar processes for each other. He sits near me till I'm fully back in waking consciousness, the changes beginning to settle in. I have no way to explain everything that's gone on during the session.

The realization of some core change, an elusive, easeful difference in my sense of self, sends flutters of excitement through me. Hints of a possible future without the splits, the anger, the sense of coercion I feel now drift into consciousness. I don't see the steps between here and there, but for once I believe they're possible.

Okay, I'll say it: I want more.

\*\*\*

"Instructions for floor processes are
not guided imagery,
nothing to do with
imagining in the mind.
They suggest bodily form, metaphors
for a state we
once inhabited,
still do
at some level.
They re-create certain
conditions of physical development,
embodied poetry;
enable us to assemble
once again in consciousness,
through our bodies,
a moment when we made a choice
we want to re-examine now. "

## Your protection is your prison.

When I was in elementary school, I used to take long walks in Orinda, the East Bay town where I grew up. It's a beautiful place, all hills and oaks and grasses, and we lived on a magical narrow winding street at the foot of a hill that dropped down to Berkeley on the other side. Canon Drive is a one-and-a-half-mile long dead end with a canyon cracking its final third; oaks overhang it, rhododendron and laurel, bay and oleander line it. Houses are set back among Monterey pines and spruces and aged deciduous vegetation.

I don't know when I started walking this street, and from there all over Orinda, for pleasure and solace and private renewal, but I was quite young. I learned to read early, and I remember climbing up the canyon at the end of the road, feeling daring and thoroughly at home making my way from rock to rock in the slippery creekbed, sitting among spiderwebs and muddy roots of trees with a book or a notebook, writing or reading or wandering with the sound of running water in my ears. It seemed to me there were worlds around me that few others perceived, and I liked being undisturbed in their space.

I still love my training runs best alone on trails through hills with trees and water. What's not always clear, though, is whether this is purposeful action toward something important that I need, or away from what I perceive as problems. It makes a difference.

*

"Doing it 'better,'
in movement terms, is about
using less effort.
This doesn't mean
'better'
as in
judgment–
it just means a more
pleasing quality of movement.
Don't rush.
Increased effort happens so that you
won't feel.
When you want
information,
decrease effort,
slow down. "

## Floor work: "how can I find you if you don't go inside?"

Anything that troubles me, anything I wonder about, any current issue whose history I want to explore or whose course I might like to change: floor work can suggest insights. My body carries not only the history of the thing, but also potential for new movement, new patterns. I can begin with any aspect of my past and turn it toward a desirable future. It's a matter of bringing the matter to consciousness, and then noticing what my tissues and bones do in relation to it.

"With very slow movements, explore turning your head to one side—toward anything desirable to you. Note where the movement stops, where the barriers to fluid motion are. Note what allows you to move past them and continue the movement."

Sometimes it's a thought, or releasing a thought; sometimes it's an infinitesimal movement of another part of me, that allows the movement to continue. What's fascinating is noticing, being with the process.

"Bring your head slowly back to center. Now in the same direction, explore turning your head *away from* the other side-away from something undesirable. Note the difference in quality of movement, in the location of the 'speed bumps,' when you are moving *toward* something you want, and when you move *away from* something undesirable. Which is easier? Which is more habitual? Which is more in keeping with how you were designed to move?

"There are no 'accurate'
memories, only embedded
experience; there are no
experiences you've participated in which are not
to some degree created by you.
As far as you are concerned,
there are no events—
because everyone's experiences of an event
—everyone's memories—
are different.
there are no
accurate memories, only
your perceptions."

"Whatever is in
the child's field of perception
at a moment of overwhelm
retroactively becomes assigned
equal
causality.
The younger we are when we
make a rule about 'always'
or 'never,' the more parts of ourselves we recruit
to make sure the
command is carried out,
and the more of our potential
becomes unavailable."

Ah. It's a matter, then, not only of noticing and wondering, but of feeling alignment with design.

*

Orinda, California, 1959. I am six. My father sits me on his lap—he's wearing a Sunday suit, and we're on the big green easy chair in the living room. While my mother makes dinner in the next room, he plays games with me. We're having fun. But then in his enthusiasm he begins to tickle me. I know we will both regret this. I've had accidents before. I squeal "no" and try to squirm away. But he holds me tightly, not letting me get away, and tickles me harder and harder, though I'm yelling and kicking, and finally I wet my pants.

He pushes me away and swears, half at my mother, half at me. "Go to your room!" he shouts. "We're going to have to get this suit cleaned now—bring me a cloth to wipe myself off!" And my mother does, looking after me as I scurry to my room, her expression telling me it's too bad this has happened, too bad I couldn't have handled myself better.

The feeling of the tickling, the hard holding and the exploding bladder; the smell of Dad's shaving cream; the sound of the mixer going in the kitchen; my father's maleness, my mother's femaleness, my own smallness and my shock that my father should be so angry at me for something he did to me—all these take on a luminosity as clear as if I had a full-grown adult mind. *Wait. Wait. Mom—somebody—listen! He made this happen! He did this himself and he's mad at me! Why is it okay for him to be angry and punish me?*

"The younger we are, the more
any 'always' or 'never' rule
becomes the basis of other
rules,
the foundation
of an inverted
pyramid of behaviors,
where at the bottom, the point, you
have original perceptions
and rules to deal
with them.
Then other rules and perceptions build on those."

Fierce, uncomprehending, I reorganize myself from the inside out. I make a rule, flashing a light on the situation now and forever so that everything is altered: if he's going to be this way, all right then: I'll make sure he can't get to me. From this moment forward, I—the small female—will withhold myself from the big male in power so he can't do this to me ever again. I'll hide my vulnerable self from him forever. He can't tickle me, he can't hurt me, he can't punish me for something he did himself, because I won't be there, even when I'm there. And I'll always know how wrong—how unfair—his punishments are, even when he's certain he's right.

At six years old, I have no idea of the implications of this decision, no idea what it will mean for me, for my father, for our relationship, for all my relationships with men (including the male God of my church) for the next thirty years. But it's irrevocable at that moment, imprinted in all my cells: to prevent this from ever happening again, I'll always acquiesce on the outside, while from the inside I'll *never* let them know how I feel.

*

"We believe the opposite gender is
what we think we aren't,
inspires fear , shame, and jealousy
(energy that  shrinks away from, not permitting entry).
Same-gender material is
what we believe the other gender isn't,
inspires judgment
(energy bounces off,
goes back into us
making us shrink from inside).
Shame, fear, and jealousy
are created by the fact
that souls don't have gender
but the body does."


"Healing alters underlying judgments.
It's not healing
if all that's changing is
the strategy
you use. In practical terms, your
strategies are always successful, always
create the predicted outcome; but
in terms of healing, they
merely mask what needs to be addressed."

Another process of discovery and release: "Call to mind the powers that you believe belong to the other gender and not to you."

*What powers males have that I don't are all socially constructed,* I tell myself, an obedient academic of the nineties fully able to recite postmodern feminist theory. *There are no inherent powers males have that I don't.*

But in my guts (literally!—there's a hard groaning in my guts when I feel what is stored there about this question) I discover that I believe men have the power to make the rules, even unfair and untrue ones—and they have the power to demand obedience, even when they lie.

"The powers you believe belong to the other gender are those you're not responsible for. You give them these powers because you dislike obligations."

*Wait a minute!*

"Victim requires victimizer. What's the payoff for being a victim?"

*Oh, shut up. I am not a victim.*

"Choose a partner whose power isn't the same as yours. Sculpt them to show your beliefs about what it means that the power is theirs and the obligation is yours."

*Here, partner. Let me sculpt you so that you're male, and you're making rules, and—*

*—oh—it's true—I do believe I am obligated to obey. I see that in the way I shape you.*

"Now, sculpt your partner to represent how you overcome their power."

---

"What matters isn't your circumstance, it's

what you make of it.

It's about choosing

and then absorbing

the vibrations that accrue

or appear

around your decision."

*I don't.*

*I just avoid them. Stay away. Pretend we're invisible to each other. Hide.*

*That helps me a lot, doesn't it?*

"Now show how you get even about your obligations."

*I'm full of contempt. I hate them. But I still comply. I just hide how angry I am.*

"Make your partner into a composite of the previous three shapes. You can see how you make life harder for yourself because of your beliefs about the other gender."

*The sculpture I make of my partner is rigid, rejecting, distancing. This is damning: what it shows me is that I'm the one who cuts off flow, exchange, give and take.*

"Notice where in your body you're holding. There's a reason for it. Now, paying attention to your body's messages, ask what you have to do in the presence of the other gender?"

I tense up, pull inward, in a dozen spots all over myself.

*What I have to do in the presence of the other gender is be on guard. Not show myself.*

"What do you need from the other gender?"

*What do I need? Nothing. Nothing, thank you.*

But then there's a tug in the direction of my left side.

*Well, okay. I'd like something—enough kindness and presence that I don't have to be on guard. Can relax. Can feel easy. That would be something.*

"At what distance do you keep that?"

*Off to the right and forward. Several feet.*

"What's the rule about distance?"

"Integrated Awareness, as it has been developed
and as it expands,
is based upon the ability of each individual
to verify the relevance and truthfulness
of the material for themselves.
One of our very few assumptions is that
if all humans do it or experience it,
it's part of the Architect's Design.
The universal human experiential behavior of
resistance
though painful to the person
and frustrating to everyone else
serves the function
of reaffirming to all parties
that we each have choice—
that this is a quantally-based planet,
with all interactions
a function of free will.
In our struggles against that which we do not like,
we not only demonstrate again
our possession of choice under all circumstances,
we also infer that we had some choice
in the creation of that which we resist."

*The rule is: stay there. I'm not going to tell you what I'm really thinking, not going to reveal my judgments. We can still interact but you won't know how far and how deep my judgment is against you for making me hide...*

"What judgment about yourself does this reflect?"

About myself? Huh? *I don't want to answer that question.*

"How does this distance, the distance at which you keep what you need from the other gender, compare to the distance of other intimate relationships?"

*Be quiet. Leave me alone.*

"What effect does this distance have on your significant other? Is he happy? Does he want more or less distance?"

*I don't want to go there.*

"How is this distance in relationship like your relationship with community, and like your relationship with Source? What's the price of admission you ask for a relationship?"

*I'm not listening very well. I'm not willing to answer these questions any more.*

"Change the distance. Choose to change it. With a heart opening. Make a gesture from head to sacrum that opens the heart. Or by moving your sternum forward, so that the back of your heart expands."

*You must be kidding.*

"If you don't take responsibility, you'll never get to forgiveness."

*Shutup. I don't want to talk about this.*

*Maybe I'll just go to sleep.*

\*

"As kids, we feel everything
and don't know how to handle it,
don't know what to do about the feelings.
We construct 'right' and 'wrong'
to inhibit ourselves.
The design intent for the mind (mental body)
is to make predictions of future reality
based on current accumulated experience.
If physical survival is in question,
the distinction between friend and foe is pivotal.
In societal frames, 'right' and 'wrong'
—rules—

come to predominate.
We make up rules
to manage  overwhelming feelings.
In spiritual terms, the essence of changing the rules
is to succeed in identifying
the discrepancies between prediction and experience—
to allow the self to see
how much more to the Self there is."

Elko, Nevada, 1961. We are traveling from California to Utah to visit grandparents as we do every year, my parents, my older brother, my little sister, my new baby brother and I. In the Nevada desert, the sky we drive toward in our new blue Plymouth station wagon is black and swollen. I'm in the back seat (this is long before the days of seat belts), a cooler and suitcases piled next to me. Suddenly we hit the black, and the sky erupts. Lightning blinds us, thunder sears our ears, we are swimming in the downpour. My father cries out my mother's name. The car swerves, fishtails, dives off the road, somersaults twice in the mud. We are scattered everywhere, my father's foot severed by his flight through a window, my mother's back broken, my brothers covered with blood and mud.

I'm conscious and upright, so authorities gather information from me about who we are, where we were going, whom to contact. My father's life is saved by a truck driver who knows how to apply a tourniquet. My sister and I spend the next six weeks with grandparents while my parents regain enough strength in the hospital to travel home. For a year, a live-in nurse cares for us. I feel myself the responsible one, the oldest healthy person in the family. I'm always a little anxious, always a little afraid that my parents won't recover, that things will be like this forever. I want attention. I put out feelers for ways to earn it. I find ways to help hold things together, alleviate the grownups' discomfort. I do well in school, earn praise for my responsibility and sensibility. I'm a dependable girl, a smart helper, an achiever: I begin to see how to be "good."

*

"The better skilled you are at
'right'
and 'wrong,'"
the more
skilled you are at
anger..."

"Our habit of abandoning
ourselves, and
our preference for
judging, have resulted
in social rules
and institutions.
Roles make you less
of yourself, make you less authentic,
less congruent in
energy
and structure."

"The very act of judgment
has disastrous effects
on the flow of energy.
It can be a positive judgment, even;
merely predicting or assigning worth or value
stops energy,
prevents spontaneous perception."

"Sitting there now,"—more instructions for floor work— "put your head in a position that is 'the right way.'"

I know this one. I know "right" from a very young time. My head sits rigidly forward, chin up, face set. Face pulled forward in a pucker—and I feel the same pucker in my pelvis, too, a micro-tuck that stops anything from flowing.

"Come to standing. Walk around in a way that's "right.""

There's a set quality to my back and shoulders, my gaze straight ahead and narrow.

"Go around and look at each other. Talk to each other."

Very polite, I am, to the people I meet, who look like strangers, all of them, though we have now been in workshop for several days together and some of them were friends when I was here before. They don't look friendly now.

"Listen to this: it's cocktail party noise, anxiety-based pretense. When you're being 'right,' you're the least of yourself."

The least of myself?

I'm listening. I'm hearing all this, and feeling the falseness of "right," but in my guts I'm also busy making connections about far more than this process in this classroom. A large part of teaching professional writing—of all academia—is instruction about what's "right." And a large percentage of my life—way more than half, I'll wager—has been living out that same instruction in arenas as widespread as school and class selection, choice of neighborhood, clothes and entertainment, marital status and family size. *Right.* So okay, it's not the best of me. But how am I supposed to live differently, when being "right" has mattered so much in every choice I've made thus far?

---

"Hope clouds perception, fear
blocks it. Hope
summons 'right,' fear
predicts 'wrong.'
If you
can operate without hope
or fear for
just ten seconds, you can know
anything you want to. When
fear diminishes, clarity
rises.
And with clarity comes power.
So you become relentless in your consciousness.
Clarity, power, and relentlessness
transmute into compassion
whenever you add love."

"Now arrange yourself, begin walking, in a way that is 'the wrong way.'"

"The wrong way" for me is ugly, crippled. Not rebellious—I don't even think about rebellion, though that might be "wrong" for others. What comes up for me is "ugly." It's wrong to be ugly, wrong to be misshapen, wrong to look bad. I have all kinds of judgments against "wrong," and they all circle around "ugly."

I go that way, hunchback and clawed and out of balance, and my face congeals in a grimace.

"Now go visit each other again."

Across the room I see Becca. Her "wrong" is almost exactly like mine. I go to her, because frankly I'm embarrassed. For some of the others, "wrong" is cocky, sassy, even seductive. I like seeing them. But I'm ugly, and I shouldn't be seen. I assume Becca feels the same kind of embarrassment, and we say to each other like two teenagers having a bad hair day, "Look at us. We're the same, aren't we?" The implication is: it won't last; we can stand to be together just because it won't last. We laugh. We are allies in "wrong," and it's not a true friendship.

"Notice the difference? The quality of talk and interaction is different. I actually like you better this way. It's quieter noise. For some of you it's more embarrassed but more authentic. For others of you it's a lot more fun. It's still not your best, though. In every event you're just less of yourself, not 'the least.' Now try arranging yourself, try walking, in a way that is neither right nor wrong."

It takes me a minute to shake off the feeling of "wrong" and rearrange myself. *Neither. Neutral.* My shoulders relax, my face unpinches. What a relief. I feel interest in things outside myself,

"If you want to know what's happening
in any human
interaction, measure by
energy: what's going
from where to whom, and what kind.
Earth is a composite of consciousness and energy.
When we're sure that we're
right,
we're drawing energy in;
when we're angry or guilty, it's going out.
Shame's energy is directed
inward;  guilt's energy is
directed outward,
like passive aggressive
anger.
The energy of arrogance
denies Source,
holds everything back,
includes a preference
for others' pain
and for being in judgment...
The energy of
excellence
invites
no projection,
holds nothing back,
commits wholly. "

allowed to have natural curiosity because I don't have to conform to a standard. This contains ease. It's about no rules, no coercives. It lets me like myself, to walk this way. It's about who I am when I'm allowed.

I'm shocked at what a difference it makes—what a difference it might make in the way my students write, in the way my children respond, in the way I swim through my whole life. I suspend judgment so seldom.

\*\*\*

"Ask for as much information
as the guest is willing
to give you.
Establish in your awareness and in your hands
the pieces you can already
tune in to–
the where of the
physical complaint,
what you know  of its vibrational relation
to other levels of consciousness.
You may or may not
need to touch the exact location they specify
–IA doesn't care too much
about that.
Let one hand go neutral,
find where else your guest has this vibration.
These other sites are connected–
but it's not cause/effect.
Do not assign causality.
There's no such thing
as one-point causality; causality
is a function
of time and position.
It's appropriate to take as a working frame
merely that all parts of the vibrational pattern
are connected."

## Energy and consciousness—that's all there is.

When I was introduced to Integrated Awareness at the
massage school, Marilyn Graham instructed us in a basic protocol:

*Find out the person's request. It can be anything: a new job; a*
*better relationship; a healed illness; an improved emotional state.*

*Now, be present in your own body. Be vulnerable, open your*
*heart. This is not just something I'm saying: vulnerability is a real tool,*
*tangible in the body.*

*Alter your state; healing is most exalted in an expanded state.*
*There are tools to help you achieve this. They are not mystical or*
*mysterious, but findable in the body, learnable.*

*Now, give your hands the intent to be effective, to find answers.*
*Let one hand go neutral at the place of primary complaint. Find*
*where other parts of the guest match this vibration. It's appropriate to*
*take as a working frame that all parts of the vibrational pattern are*
*connected.*

*Now, link in everywhere that's interesting. Prioritize. Ask,*
*"What's helpful here? Direct or indirect intervention? Should I put*
*my hands in a new position or leave them here? How does my own*
*body feel? Under my hands, do I feel a flow between the two*
*locations? What is their path back to balance? Should I make this*
*energy more or less, or just be with it?"*

At the massage school, trying it out with other students, all of
this felt eminently reasonable, possible, feasible. I begin in my very
first Touchstone workshop to put my hands on people with intent
to help them allow changes in themselves. This pleases me greatly,

"It's appropriate
to ask as an early question,
'Have you had medical care for this?'
If not, check your intuition
concerning whether or not to refer your guest
right now, or to suggest
that they get medical attention
before they return."

"Curiosity is indispensable to the worker
because it links discovery with responsibility.
To the student, 'I'm doing this
because I'm curious' means
'I'm doing this to learn—
with the freedom to err
on an equal playing field.'"

partly because it's taken for granted that I *can* do this—that if I'm human and awake, I can sense with my hands and be of assistance according to what I learn. I like that this becomes a component of self-identification.

But I also like doing this because I'm curious. At the massage school I laid hands on people with various intents: Swedish stimulates muscles. Shiatsu contacts the meridians in the body, opening them or balancing them. Craniosacral therapy senses subtle body rhythms and restores them. Here, though, at Touchstone, no one thing—and anything—is expected to happen under my hands. I feel for what there is to feel, assuming that information awaits my perception and that in the information itself is the instruction about what to do with it. But first, it helps if I'm in my body, "present."

*

"Whether you want to be seen,
or to do better,
to feel more capable,
or to tackle any issue:
show up.
More presence
will fulfill your wish."


"Bodies don't lie.
Divinely conceived and created,
elegantly endowed,
your body is the only thing you can count on
every time
to tell you the absolute truth.
In your body is the ability to know
whether anything you ask about
is or is not in keeping with your life purpose;
in keeping with a state of health for you;
or in keeping with welcoming consequences.
Ask anything,
and your body will answer."

**When you want to have the most impact on your own or anyone else's life, you bring together as many parts of yourself, from wherever and whenever as you can. The more present you are, the better.**

We explore what it means to "be here"—to be "present." I'm under the skylight in this calm, blue-carpeted room, still testing the effects of this work on myself. The space is deliberately designed to be safe, quiet, comfortable, but enlivening. I rarely fall asleep, unless I'm resisting information. Right now sun lights a square of space just beyond my reach, and we all lie waiting for instructions.

"Lying on the floor, note three parts of yourself—three areas in your physical body—that are not available for authenticity. You know they're not available because they're tight, you're holding them, you don't think about them when you move and they don't move of themselves."

Such places are all over me. First, my face—cheeks, jaws. Once I find them, I notice how stretched they feel, how *arranged*. But there are also such places in my shoulders. There's a distinct deep spot up near my neck on the left, about the size of a quarter, that's almost always sore.

"Note more, if there are more."

Well. How long do we have to go on with this? It's embarrassing. More in my face—under my chin, around my ears. I *squinch*. And down my back—oh, all over the place. I make note of about two dozen places. They're easy to find. I had no idea I was such a mass of knots. This is interesting, because I'm a healthy runner, a

"Patterns of thinking or
feeling or
believing manifest themselves
in our structure.
Taking note of our structural
patterns
gives us insight into
the beliefs that run our lives.
Changing energy
will change structure, and
vice versa."

"This process isn't
to give you formulaic
answers. IA never does.
It's to help you remember
the choice you already made."

"Tightening or
holding or
stopping altogether
generally indicate negative response or fear;
expanding, relaxing, release
of pressure
generally indicate a
positive response or acceptance."

wise eater and weight watcher since my early twenties. You'd think I'd be so bodily aware there'd be no walled-off place in my structure, no place I'm not.

Think again.

"Now exaggerate the unavailability, and know that it's okay. It's okay that they're not available. Hold them. Keep them tight."

Making them tighter than they were makes me laugh again. There are so many. It's such an effort. And I'm so comforted by that phrase, "it's okay," that I feel the effort is hardly needed any more. Which tells me plenty about why the empty places are there at all: it's because I think somebody judges me not okay.

*Who would that be?*

"But as you hold them, note what places are left after you've found the ones that are unavailable. In other words, find the parts of you that *are* available."

Oh. There really are some. Look—when I'm not paying attention, my left first finger is just all there, neither empty nor tight. So are the back of my right eye and both my upper arms— they feel normal, not hurting and not held back, not resisting, not defending, but sort of actively relaxed, ready for me. Allies.

I find an available spot under my left shoulder blade (I call it a wingbone). Right great toe. Hands—palms of hands. And certain parts of my brain also, just agreeably there, I can feel them, serving me whether I know it or not.

Cool. Okay, I'll choose those.

"And send that availability, slowly, as they'll allow you to, into the places that you're holding. Watch them relax. Watch what happens. Some won't let 'availability,' or 'presence,' in.

———

"Re-wire your body.

There is always

choice, always the chance

to change. "


"Attend to your heart.  If the back opens, or needs to,

forgive yourself.

If the front,

forgive (an)other(s)."

But some will. And the more that do, the more there are that will. Let yourself fill as far as you can."

We take our time. It feels so different to let my jaw relax I almost fear for my safety. How can I be all right if my jaw's relaxed?

Other things happen when the tightness in my jaw releases. My back meets the floor differently; I wonder how it will feel to stand. My tongue moves—could it actually be getting fatter? My cheeks expand, my whole face changes—I can sense it, a loosening from inside. I must look entirely different. What'll my husband say?

My heart goes big and then, surprisingly, my eyes fill with tears. If this is what authenticity is, I remember it. I roll over, stretching, loving the square of sun now directly on my back. "Availability" fills me up. It's old and familiar, a relief. It tastes of oak trees, of green hills, of walking and writing. I recognize it: Oh, friend of my favorite days! I have you back! Welcome!  It's me.

Delicious.

*

"A mantra for the return to regular life:
When you go back, you'll exhibit changes.
Part of the time,
your significant others will be thrilled
to see the changes in you.
On occasion,
they'll just look at you and say 'huh?'
The rest of the time, you'll get
NIMBY-'not in my back yard.'
Be prepared for that.
There are some ethical ways to handle it.
First:
model your changes
by neither advertising nor hiding them.
Don't do pretense.
Second, allow your loved ones their reactivity.
Don't try to control
or even influence
their reactions.
The first moment you see them
will be the most important.
Keep your heart open. No defenses.
Create in yourself an appreciation
for multiple simultaneous idiosyncratic realities.
Welcome to planet earth.
Don't resist."

**'Becoming more aware' equals 'becoming more responsible for,' and 'more responsible for' means you belong.**

At home between IA workshops and immersed in the experience of floor work, I begin to test the benefits of movement as exploration. Sometimes I'm expanded by my private floor sessions—periods of moving, noticing quality and direction and shape of movement. At the very least, by the time I stop I've stretched and recruited every major muscle group in my body. I feel energized. The thing about which there seems to be no question is that the processes *do have an effect.*

Certain questions start them most profitably for me and allow me to notice aspects of myself I've not been aware of before: where am I—physically, emotionally, energetically—right now? What shape or posture represents a composite of what's going on for me right now? What would be more aesthetically pleasing? What would help me to be or do more of what I want? What rules are stopping me, and how shall I change them for more consistent expansion? Almost always I notice the stiffness of my face first, and when I relax that, other parts of me shift as well. Most of the time I don't bother putting names to what's happening. I just feel wholly there, and sometimes I spend the rest of the day in a state of happiness and strength which has benefits for everyone I meet.

During good moments, I consider the movement a devotion. It seems that movement is a thing I could do every day, could should would. A good move. Move. Good.

"What would you risk much in order to have?
If there were a place in your life that could be
easier or better, where would it be?
If you're standing on an edge,
your awareness spikes!
If you're pushed,
all you focus on
is the anticipated hard landing.
If you jump voluntarily,
you notice everything
all the way down."

Historically, IA training has consisted of three-year profession-al courses offered in closed groups of enrolled trainees, with week-end workshops for the public. Now the program is changing: cer-tain of us are invited to enroll as apprentices whose programs will be individualized and separately supervised, and we're invited to aim ourselves toward certification as IA teachers.

The very word "apprentice" appeals to me. It has overtones of assisted progress, directed expansion. These growing capabilities in my hands, and the cellular, consciousness-harmonic logic of these movements by which my body yields information about its own healing, won't just be flung at me pell-mell—I'll be under super-vised contract to increase awareness skills for my personal healing as well as for the purpose of transmitting these tools to others. It's the how-to of miracles made accessible. The notion of becoming a Touchstone apprentice appeals to me very much.

But—there are always "buts." One winter morning, I lie on the floor downstairs in the TV room listening to the roar of con-flicting internal voices. *If you apprentice at Touchstone—if you buy into the precepts embodied in IA—many of the reasons for your choic-es up to now may prove to be obsolete. Integrated Awareness is a way of looking at the world that will allow you to see everything different-ly: what humans are; what reality is; what's possible. You can't put hands on people with intent to assist change in consciousness and not have nearly every assumption you've ever held change as well.*

Let's face it—I'm a very ordinary English teacher, just a wife and mom. How do I tell people—family, friends, neighbors—that I can feel their energy, their consciousness, when they're hesitant to acknowledge that it exists in the first place? A whole public

"I don't have any answers.
What I have, I hope, are questions and means by which to use
tools innate in you,
designed into you
so that you could feel your desires,
make conscious choices,
have anything you want,
become a co-creator with Source."



"The more you do this work of healing,
the more you will sacrifice.
But it is not loss,
except of preconditions
on your capacity to serve."

re-education needs to happen before it's accepted in the general populace the way it's taken for granted at Touchstone that we're energy beings whose physical structure reflects and reciprocally maintains the state of all other levels of consciousness. A different paradigm, that's what we encounter at Touchstone. The tools that use touch to influence health and well-being are only barely beginning to be accepted as innately human, transmissible, and genuinely effective. What's my place here? Am I really doing any more than dabbling, satisfying a curiosity for the avant-garde, a secret need for connection through touch while habitually I will try to stay as conventional, as rule-following, as "normal" as I can be?

I listen to these voices, and I tense up, in my face first and all along the length of my back and torso, to stave off the frightening, unnamed consequence of being seen not as an innocuous instructor in a giant English department but as (sh!) a healer. Yet many places in me relax when I imagine letting go of some ancient struggle by which I believe that in order to be "good," in order to deserve life, I have to maintain externally imposed standards, evaluate people daily, hand out and follow lists of "right" and "wrong" and "supposed-to" and "must." When I imagine opening up to a worldview in which those unseen possibilities of my childhood are the real basis for action—when I imagine moving in a world where that assumption receives increased support, belief, acceptance—a scarcely sustainable lightness floats through me.

*How shall I resolve this?*

I lie on the floor, wanting my body to show me an answer, twisting a little to one side, but getting nothing.

———

"If you want to get
what you say you want,
you must not hide;
you must commit;
and you must be willing to desire."

Rolling. A little more emphatic movement.

Still, no resolution..

Face down, completely still, for a long, long time:  nothing for many  minutes, a quarter hour, nothing. I just wait.

Then, like an infusion, an explosion of strength and intensity, my entire body rises to full height. I don't even know how I get here. From the centers of the cells, absolute congruence. Certainty on all levels. Clear, uncontestable instructions: *"Recruit all your parts. Do this! Go forward!"*

So this is the beginning of commitment.

\*\*\*

*"Unconditional:*

a functional technique for touch,

a working tool,

a state you can approach with practice:

total absence of coercion.

When you're there, you're off

the time line; all sensory

patterns fall away,

are understood to be

habitual.

The more unconditional a healer is,

the more possibility for change in the guest."

## You don't get to live a life where you don't make a difference.

We practice sending energy consciously to each other, to feel the effects of our own consciousness on the work we're trying to do—the effects of our own self-imposed rules on the way we perceive. (This is how we create our own reality, always.) I'm eager to put words to the feelings in my hands. It's a matter of metaphor—like heat or tingling or prickles, or whatever images come into my consciousness.

"One of you be on the table receiving energy, one of you place hands on a body site appropriate to the wish of the one on the table. Now, in turn, let the one on the table bring in her own likely objections, and then the one who is helping intend to flavor her work with specific intentions and desires, so that you can both see how these aid or interfere with the transmission of energy."

I find it hilariously complex to attend to what's happening under my hands while my partner purposely brings in a quality of "I can't have this" and "I don't deserve it." The energy feels slippery under my palms, I can't keep hold of it. We go at it again, a little slower this time.

When I set my intent to work "unconditionally," I have a sense that there is neither time nor space. I have available to me a meditative, clean, productive blankness, a clear screen, that allows anything and everything to happen.

By contrast, when I put my hands on my partner and bring to mind an idea that the work is about myself—when I rest my self-esteem on external opinion—then a familiar quality shaped like

"Learning involves having your experience not match your expectation. The best learning happens when there's no judgment about either the expectation or the experience."

"All the data you could ever want is available to you as soon as you are willing to take responsibility for it."

an arch, a curve of tension (the way I habitually hold in my stomach), a bit too structured to allow full choice, pervades the energy.

If I add my own wish to the wish my partner has declared, mushiness invades the clarity, a kind of muddy soft cottony fill so that the clear screen is co-opted. The energy we both feel is much less productive than it is when I'm "unconditional." There's much less space there to move.

And when I hold—even privately—the idea that those I'm working with are better or worse than I am—when I separate myself from them by judgment and evaluation—it's as if a portcullis clangs down into the moat of a castle, locking me out of healing's potential unless I dive under my own judgment and surface beyond its reach.

* * *

"*Special:*
different in a way that draws attention to you
and away from everyone else
by emphasizing some perceived defect(s) in yourself.
'Special' hinders connection,
hinders excellence,
increases separation.
Insists that others
don't have what you do.
'Special' distorts."

"Don't say 'you said...'
It's not what I said, it's *what*
*you heard me say.*
It's not my own words I'm speaking
--I'm hearing your thoughts and giving them back to you.
I'm closing the thought loops
already in the room."

"What makes you 'special'? Get in position for the process: lie prone."

Half of us flop down on our bellies, the other half on our backs. I'm mildly contemptuous—don' t those people know what "prone" means? Part of what makes me 'special' is how well I know words. But I'm not about to say so.

"Make the side of you with your belly and face closer to the floor than the side of you with your back," Lansing says. Much nicer than I'd have been. I chortle into the floor.

"Now, make a movement that embodies 'special,'" he says. "Make a slight adjustment of your pelvis, foot, or little finger to show how you feel about keeping 'special' hidden."

Ah, he heard me thinking that I don't want to reveal how special I am and he's not going to let me get away with it. I'm still laughing, my left ear pressed to the floor. I pull my right knee up to my chest, turn my face so that my third eye stares straight down into the floor. Without analyzing, simply letting my body respond to the prompt, I let my pelvis drop over to the right so that my drawn-up right knee is now crossed under my left leg. Yes. That's it. That's how I feel about keeping "special" hidden.

"Good, Julie!" I hear him say. I don't know why he says this; it's obviously not about "right" or "wrong" but about "congruent" and "authentic." Whenever he says, "Good, Julie," or "That's so beautiful, Jul!" or "Right on," I'm always in an unselfconscious, quiet-minded place. He never says it when I'm performing or

"Music or math or consciousness,
'harmonic':
a sound or pitch,
or wave of light,
whose rate of vibration precisely matches
a multiple of the originating one,
and whose effect
is pleasing. It's
all numbers, frequencies
of waves of
light or sound:
energy."

anxious. And he's aware of everyone, not just me; the movement processes are designed specifically for our individual needs, not only from the conception of the workshop's theme but also in every moment, as we interpret and carry out the instructions and Lansing's teacher's eye sees what we need for further learning. At least once a workshop I believe a floor process to have been devised, and revised in the doing of it, just for me.

"Just sit," says Lansing.

That's easy.

Then, "Divide yourself into left and right halves. Let one half vibrate at a faster rate than the other." Also easy, when I consider how familiar being split has been in my life.

"Now, with these two vibrations in the two halves of your structure, find a third vibratory rate—a third harmonic—and tune yourself to that."

Find a third frequency? What, higher or lower?

This idea—that I can a) split myself, b) identify a particular vibratory experience in each half of me, and c) then create a third sensory something that includes both halves and yet is neither one—is interesting. I'm a kid with a new toy. I concentrate with the effort and pleasure of figuring it out. For fun, I peek to see everyone else's version of "find a third frequency." Disappointment!—everyone sits with their eyes closed, mostly doing what looks like nothing, although it's obvious from the varying degrees of ease and effort in their faces and body positions that they're all fully engaged. Meanwhile my own momentum is completely lost. Bummer. I won't peek again.

----

"Here
we work with the harmonics
of all the components
of our being—
expressed and discoverable
in the body,
the resonance of
all the levels of consciousness
reverberating in our bones. "

"Start with the
solution
and work backward to
the problem.
The solution is
that the physical body is
always in present time—
designed that way,
because it's a given
that other levels of consciousness won't be."

So I start over. One more time I tune half of me to one vibration—easy to begin by calling in the vibration that does everything right. It hums along, a fairly low frequency, steady, predictable, monotone, monochrome, like vanilla ice cream. Not particularly interesting or intense, but not *bad*. We're not judging here. We're just noticing.

I focus then on the other half, the vibration I go to secretly, the one I hide. Definitely faster, maybe thirty to fifty percent higher. Definitely more exciting. Just enough variation to draw strange attractors in. There's an undercurrent, perhaps, of fear. I might get caught. I realize that at this frequency, I love. At the other, I just keep on working.

So I'm lying on the floor in this safe and expanded place, this blue-carpeted light classroom, playing with two unlike vibrations, ordinary and extraordinary, mundane and miraculous, the story of my life. (Maybe of everyone's life, and I haven't known it.) And I'm supposed to create a third vibration, make something new. This is the planet of polarity and paradox; transcending duality is how we expand, how we create. Do I go for a higher or lower frequency? What kind of vibration will embrace both parts of me? I feel like laughing.

"Don't analyze. Let your body tell you."

And it does. I can feel myself checking not just different frequencies but whole different measuring cues. My body (or my energy?) seems to want to arrive at—well, something neither higher nor lower. It's different than either of the other two energetics I'm holding. It's like a full guitar chord riff instead of a one-string melody, a three-dimensional iridescence replacing one flat piece of

"We've all experienced days,

circumstances,

people,

in relation to whom or which

everything is easy,

or hard.

Most of the confusing, contradictory explanations for this

are simply projections of our own inner conflicts and reactions.

'Goes easily'

or 'goes with difficulty'

is overwhelmingly a function of timing.

'Goes easily'

means the rest of the universe wants what you want

simultaneously.

'Goes hard'

means the rest of the universe

wants to you have it

at another juncture.

Remember: insist on having something, and you will

though you may no longer wish it."

construction paper, a seven-course meal following a fast. It's got more dimensions, more flavor, than either half alone.

"Let the two halves be male and female. Run up and down the scale and note how many male and female tunings there are for you." Something I've never thought of before: that different parts of me could be tuned one way, other parts tuned another, such that all the parts that are tuned similarly are harmonically linked. Not just within me, either, but between me and others, between all of us and Source. Complex implications for healing surface and fade, to reappear, I hope, at appropriate moments.

"Let these two halves of you be anything you want: your health and everybody else's; current time and past time; performance vs. authenticity. Travel through these possibilities. Note differences between the two halves in each case. Note where in your body the different vibrations occur. Pause to create a third harmonic for each pairing, and tune both halves to it, to transcend seeming incompatibilities."

In some instances, what "transcends seeming incompatibilities" is easy and pleasurable. When I check "my health" (a strong, earthy energetic) against "everyone else's" (less strong, more like the "ordinary" I took on earlier), I can make a third harmonic (wide and yellow) that pulls everybody out on the running field with me, lifts them into the sunshine, feels the joy of moving fast, all of us together in a well-run race.

Yet other times I can't get to a third harmonic. I get tied up in rule-knots. Rule-nots. As if my body were saying, "Hold it, Jul—trust me. It's not time yet."

"Practice tuning yourself
to things you don't understand in others,
and instinctively
you will discover and choose tools you need."

"It's not the tool
but the tool-user
that matters,
not the paint but
the painter, not the adze
or hammer
but the carpenter..."

"What we're giving you here
is a menu.
No one is expected
to consume every item on it.
If you try to sample
everything, you're not getting
what you need."

We work in pairs to find the comfort zones for each of us as healing agents. We explore the spectrum between wanting to fix the symptom (probably the least useful activity a healer can engage in) and going in timespace to the very origin of the difficulty, to facilitate adjustments there (perhaps the most risky). In this way we determine the range between "what's the least I'm willing to do?" and "what's more than I'm willing to do?"—the range in which we're most comfortable at the moment, the range in which we're most successful, most ethical and most safe. Lansing suggests we check this every time we start a session, till it becomes a habit. The range will change from day to day and over time; checking it out is a good way to stay in tune with ourselves and our abilities.

He suggests we put the fingertips of our same-gender hand on our solar plexus to get a sense of where our comfort zone is with power and with healing. Toward my left I find a clear "I don't know enough about structure to rearrange someone's bones" line; to the right there is a quick clear "I can feel energy" spot, surprisingly expansive. We do a brief process with each other to confirm what we discover. Afterward, Faith says, "Not knowing how to do it was not a reason to stop." Elaine says, "My zone markers were so low and so high that it was the same." Patricia says, "When I remembered that I was to shut down, I gave up, and when I gave up, I expanded." Her partner Ed says, "I don't know what I'm doing," and his neighbor, Dave, punches him lightly: "That's postgraduate work!"

\*

"Every student reveals

his or her own

best mode for learning.

The IA teacher will remember

that there are functionally infinite numbers of ways

to direct guests in the dance of their own learning,

will allow the energy of the moment

to suggest the steps,

will use the students' own desires

as the impetus and forward motion."

"If a transformative movement process can take five minutes or less, what is it we're preparing ourselves to create here when we have lifetimes? What are your intentions? What's our purpose in doing this?"

Ed ventures, "To go home. To feel at home and to help people not do weird things." People laugh, but Lansing says, "The reason for the weirdness is the belief in separation. The degree of healing is related to the frequency, duration, and constancy with which you feel completely connected."

*

"How do you spot choice in your guest?" Lansing asks. "How do you know when they've hit a choice point?"

Mark says, "You follow the map. When energy can go where it hasn't gone before, they've made a new choice."

Rajyo says, "There's relaxation in the whole system."

Faith says, "It's as if they've cut the moorings."

Elizabeth says, "There's a still point at choice; there's expansion just after.'"

Lansing says, "Yes, it's an active stillness. No insurmountable barriers. No mandatories and no prohibitions. The buildup to choice is a greater and heavier sense of responsibility. When they finally do choose, I feel a lessening of that urgency. When they make the choice I feel relief, and as the choice spreads, I feel dismissed."

*

"Languaging
is the mind's most reliable way
of reshaping itself to win the approval of others.
It is simultaneously dependent
upon the physical body for expression,
the emotional self for inspiration,
and the passage of energetic waves
for its medium of transmission.
Accordingly,
language usually bridges
what is
and what's supposed to be.
Much of what you hear in the Integrated Awareness world
is devoid
or minimally possessed
of 'what should be'
so that the way in which words are used
is startling—
uncomfortable at times."

Carol Lessinger, a teacher who graduated from an earlier IA training, comes to Utah several times a year. For some months early in my apprenticeship, she invites me to assist her while she gives group table sessions when she's in town. During the sessions, as during workshops and classes at Touchstone, I notice what my hands want to do, what they feel. I follow Carol's direction but I also gather my own impressions and work from my own intuition.

The guests' energetics differ as widely as their faces and voices and body types. Lansing has said, "If you're depressed or bored, just get interested in how other people organize themselves. It'll take you a long time to run out of material if you do." As a writing teacher I've loved reading my students' stories for precisely this reason. Here, doing hands-on work, I find another way to read people, another way to know their stories.

Gradually I begin to work with clients (or "guests") on my own. When I work with one guest whom I see often, I rarely say anything, though what's happening under my hands is intense and powerful. She responds dramatically even though I don't speak. We find ourselves in a dance of movement and support that comes to a natural, energizing rest point.

But when I work with another frequent guest, I am often moved to speak aloud. In her case, the words give her permission to make a change. I ask her to bring to consciousness the origins or effects of her complaints; I draw her attention to the subtle movements in her body's responses to my questions and directions; I suggest new ways to think of her body in relation to energy, emotion, beliefs. If I don't speak, she asks me to, and I know that she

"Language is an energetic.
When you use language,
shape the words, the sound,
the self, and the hearer,
so that what is meant
is what is heard."

"If I sense that the guest
will benefit from my speaking
then I do."

doesn't believe she really feels what she feels unless I somehow verify it aloud. She always listens carefully and sometimes answers, but if she doesn't, afterward when we compare notes we're thrilled at how closely our perceptions correspond.

*

During the second year of my apprenticeship, Touchstone comes to Salt Lake City. Three times we present weekend IA workshops at the University of Utah; groups of about twenty attend, some of them my friends, some of them Carol's clients, some of them affiliated elsewhere. Afterward, I begin to teach floor processes to small groups of them on a regular basis, finding out for myself how invigorating it can be to create one-of-a-kind movement explorations based on students' wishes and current desires. Working on the spot, tuning energetically to the students' processes, synthesizing what I've experienced with the discovery possibilities suggested by each person's declaration in the moment, I teach my university writing classes differently also. I play more with "feeling it in the body," less with "right" and "wrong"—a risky strategy at this university! I even talk about consciousness and energy in writing. It's fun. The students seem delighted. Bringing IA to my territory does something healing and integrating for me. I feel less and less split.

*

"This is the first question we work with here:

Is the universe friend

or foe

or stranger?

You live on that line.

All your choices

come from your answer to this."

## In any context that includes Source, learning, healing, and forgiving are the same thing: acceptance.

It finally happens: I'm told I will not be re-hired to teach creative writing because of the subversive nature of some of my recently published fiction. At first I brag to friends that I'm quite able to remain present in the face of this disconcerting news. But as the implications settle in—my comfortable work habits, my reliable paycheck, my self-concept as an inspiring university writing teacher, all gone in the blink of an eye—I'm more and more upended. I begin to wish to take revenge on the new department chair who made this decision. I think of ways to blow him up. Him or me. Unabomber plots. Grenades in his office, in his car, in his dog's pen—or mine. What am I going to do now, career-wise? I'm lost.

Well, *I'm* lost, but *he's* an idiot, a self-righteous bumpkin, proof that the universe isn't made up of my friends, but my very real foes. Somebody needs to pay. I have to…do something!

In class at Touchstone, the group begins a movement process whose aim is to facilitate forgiveness, letting go, setting up new avenues for connection. There are plenty of choice points where we can rest rather than continue the process. We can choose to forgive or not. We can choose whether to continue the connection or not. We can choose what kind of connection we want.

It's obvious: my job situation is the perfect choice. If I'm at Touchstone to heal, then it's time for me to forgive, let go, move on. So during the process, at each choice point I push through: okay, I'll forgive; okay, I'll continue the connection with the

"If you feel coerced,
stop.
You choose to change or not,
to heal or not;
to lower resistance,
stop.
If you try everything, if you force
anything,
you're messing up. Staying
with your process
is the point."


"Timing is everything.
If you don't want to maintain a compassionate
connection,
the universe will still
support you.
Your sense of freedom to stop at any time
is more important than forgiveness at this moment. Soul
is delighted
when you make a choice of any kind,
prefers that you choose
than that you feel
immobile
or coerced."

department, with academia; okay, I'll take the most beneficial connection, whatever that is.  I never get any "no, I refuse this" signals from my body (and I've had those—they're unmistakable stops and contractions and blockages—I'd recognize them if they came). But I'm not feeling liberation and expansion either—not really, not yet.

When we're instructed to stand, to feel gravity through the newly rearranged matrix and to feel how the new forgiveness feels, I get a clear message: *no coercives, Julie; no coercives.* I stop everything to listen. It isn't a voice. It's just the words in my head. *No coercives.*

I stand still to let it in. It takes me a few minutes to get it. But it becomes clearer as the seconds pass. Listen, Jul. You don't have to forgive this. You don't have to go on with the process of letting it go.  I stand still in my corner of the classroom and listen and let it sink in: *no coercives. No coercives.* I stop the process here. It's not startling or melodramatic. It's just kind, unconditional, vastly generous: a choice point. *My* choice. I have plenty of choices about what to do next, a wide-open field. The future is mine to author. I'd rather pay attention to that than be stuck in revenge, any time.

*

"There are no such things as

events.

Only perceptions.

To change things,

change

your labels, and assume

you're part of everything you experience."

## Don't quit and don't run.

Even so, uncertainty besets me. About my firing, my husband says, "It's the best thing to happen to you. You've been wanting out for a long time."

One of my past teachers says, "You outgrew that job years ago. The door of the cage is standing open. Fly through it."

Lansing has said, "When a change like this happens, don't try to put your life back the way it was. Ask yourself how you want it to be."

I find part-time work at another university and am amazed to discover how little I care about it, how little passion there is for me there. It's a fine university, but the teaching of freshman composition doesn't have the flavor of necessity and outrageousness that the teaching of creative writing at a stiflingly conservative school seemed to have. Odd that the very thing I resented gave fire to my work, odd to discover that defiance fueled me so. Week by week, it's clearer and clearer that I hung on to that job for reasons that are old, stale, out of date.

My passion is no longer in teaching university writing. My protection—a paycheck at a time when my family needed one, in a field (teaching writing in a university setting) where I felt expanded at the time and not split—became my prison. Now it's time to show up for the next thing, to release the old habits from my physical and emotional and energetic bodies, reach out for all the data I'll take responsibility for, use it to expand to "be everything I came here to be" instead of making myself smaller—use it to forgive, to let go of coercives, and to heal.

*

"Either you die
of the lessons you haven't
learned,
or
one final time
you die from learning all your lessons."

"Bring to mind a dream you've always had but never done anything about."

I choose—well, I'm confused about what to choose. Surely I've done something about every dream I ever had. And after many table sessions and more time on the floor, I feel much less angry than I used to about the ones I haven't brought to full flower, much more willing to be soft and patient about the ones I still hold though they don't yet manifest.

But today, as I lie here once again on the floor, the number of times I've not done more seeps into my consciousness as an accusation. Maybe I've come to kinder terms with the status of each desire, but I see with horrible clarity now that much of the time I've settled for the small, safe thing I thought was "right." No wonder the larger, wilder wishes haven't come true: I always pulled back. Didn't go to Berkeley for graduate school but stayed in Utah. Taught part-time, not full time. Didn't publish any more after a certain point. Didn't teach radical creativity at home. Didn't take responsibility for changing constricting conditions but blamed others, even hated them. Didn't didn't didn't—from here, suddenly, my choices look woefully unexpanded. I'm overwhelmed at how much time I've lost, how I walled my own self in. It looks awful. I wish I could evaporate.

I'm not at this new rough place because IA has failed me. I'm not having a relapse, am not drowning in self-pity or "specialness." On the contrary: *awareness has increased.* Just as when the immune system has been alerted to the presence of a foreign substance it leaps into action more quickly than before, now I seem to see more and more clearly how, before new choices can be made, I'll

"There's no more frequently undertaken task
with less proportional harvest
than working toward change through the mind.

The mind is the portion of consciousness
that creates coercives
and makes judgments.
The mind perpetuates
closed loop cycles
by assigning reverse cause-
effect relationships, by
'whipping the cart.'"

need to face the consequences of these smallnesses—*face* them. Maybe it's no wonder my face is always so tight: I'm resisting the extent of the truth. It looks pretty grim from here.

But there's a movement process for my discomfort.

"Surrounded by helpers, arrange your body to contain as many traces as you can of that which besets you. Let the helpers feel the vibration of those traces on all levels. Then let them give those vibrations back to you exponentially. Let them increase until you can't take in any more. Then let your helpers pour even more in. See what happens."

I'm fearful, listening to these instructions. Self-doubt and disparagement threaten to paralyze me. I don't want to be filled to overflowing with the emotional consequences of my own crummy choices. Anticipating acute discomfort, I can barely do my job as "helper." I don't think I want to be the one "helped."

I go through the motions, though, watching each member of my group and other groups in the room experience the entire process, and nobody dies, though I think the sighs of expansion I hear from those who go all the way to the end must be made up, must be a performance. "It's going to hurt," I say to myself. "It's going to be a lot of physical pain, I know it." I don't know why I'm so convinced of that, but I am.

Yet nobody runs screaming out of the room. And all those sighs! By the time it's my turn I've decided at least to yield to the process until I can't stand it—whatever happens, I'll let it go on at least that long. I'll go in curious.

And surprisingly, there's no nausea, no physical stabbing or burning or throbbing ache. I tell myself maybe it's because I'm

"The job of the mind is to discern,

compare, predict—not to avoid pain

but to improve the accuracy of our perceptions,

to tell us where more

needs to be included

in our model or reality. "

stopping the thing by the force of my mind. Maybe I'm a coward, resisting the real results.

But my group is better than that. They won't be stopped. Mind isn't so powerful over them. They pour my regret, my "I've done it all so badly!" back into me and I feel fuller and fuller, only it's not pain I'm full of. It's a quality of me, a quality I've come to recognize as *Julie,* multidimensional and interesting and rich and accepting of my smallness as if that were a component of my expansion. Fuller and fuller of Julie, I am. And at the apex, at the height of the "pouring back in," when I'm really ready not to hold one more drop of remorse and self-recrimination, the revelation comes: not "I'll never make it," not "I'll never be good enough," but "This is me, and I *can!*"

\*

"In every action,

in every choice,

in every mistake, in every effort

there are seeds of heart

and Source.

Search for the seeds

and honor them.

Love them.

Use them."

**We encourage you to seek excellence as a personal characteristic more ardently than skill.**

"Come to stand in a way that demonstrates your most intractable obstacles. Let your body take the shape of your 'no's. Holding on to those, now sit, adding the lie."

Each of us interprets this in whatever manner seems most applicable. My body takes once more my default position, the familiar stiff posture I've explored so many times at Touchstone. How tired I am of it, how ready to release it.

We move backward in time, retracing backward our developmental postures, sitting, then lying down, holding these "no"s, these lies, finally adding shape and movement for "the truth that was inherent in you as an infant. If you can't find that, add your heart," Lansing says. As I've become accustomed to doing, I don't think about it, just let my body do it, and come to standing bursting light through my chest, though I'm still cramped and stiff in my back and shoulders, my hips and hands. All of us look like this, glorious at core but in other places withheld, hidden, refused. We see each other in various degrees of contortion and discomfort, but with heart and original truth shining through, and what we see is real people, the way they are, uneven and imperfect, reaching, despite rule and role and what-we've-been-told, toward their best selves, their highest potential—for God. It's good for me, levels me, crumbles a few more layers of the wall of judgment and comparison. It makes me want to be kind.

*

"Kid Talk:

When a kid says, 'I have to,'

he means 'I don't believe you'll love me if I don't.'

'I can't' means 'I'm afraid to,'

or 'I don't have permission.'

'I trust you'

means 'God doesn't want me to hurt,

and it's your fault if I do.'

In adult terms, 'I trust you' means 'I know you

and I feel that your intention

is not to do me harm.'"


Q. "How do you know you're

not done

with your lessons?"

A. "You're still breathing."


"Never give a person his

last chance.

Always be the one

to give him his

*next* chance."

**Healing is the best revenge. If you want to balance the scales, get over it.**

"Standing, let your body take a shape representing something you've always wanted but not manifested. Now divide your body in half."

I've done this before.

Well, okay, not precisely this. Never two processes the same.

"On the gender side, make a physical movement toward what you want, but with no energy behind it, showing how your attitude toward this is 'I have to, but I don't really want to.' This is how you disavow your actions.

"On the nongender side, let your energy move but without physical action, showing 'I want to, but I can't or am afraid to.' This is how you disavow your intentions.

"Let the two disparate gestures move toward each other to the point of confusion or contradiction. Allow your partner to assist you by supporting you as you relax into a surprisingly new position showing 'This is what I *really* want."

That "relax" thing again—and when my partner supports my trunk and arms, I sink into something halfway, neither standing nor kneeling, ambivalent, uncertain. It looks like I'm still doing reticence. I let my weight rest on my partner's hands and stay with it as long as I can, to find out what this is, how to let it go. How to fix it.

But IA is not about fixing, I know that. The removal of conditions is the purpose of sacrifice; the question "what do you need

"Self-forgiveness
is a behavior
and requires the same ingredients
as any other behavior:
physical and energetic movement by intention
and acceptance of consequence.
In self-forgiveness, the heart
is physically elevated within the thoracic cavity
and energetically expanded, especially toward the back.
Of course, self-forgiveness also requires
that you be present in your body
and aware of what you're doing."


"Everything on this planet is always a matter of choice
—including perception.
We choose to see color or not,
to accept or not
the very concepts
of shape and size and dimension,
to hear sounds only through our ears
(rather than on our skin, as we do in the womb)
and as coming from only one location or not
—*to experience ourselves as connected*
*to others, or self, or Source*
—or not.
To step away from 'accepted' perceptions
is to increase possibility infinitely."

before you'll let yourself have what you say you want?" is one of the more affecting of the questions I've learned to ask during processes like this. What I receive here is support for finding out.

For a moment I can feel that what I really want is to sink to the floor in a gesture of yielding, and then to stand tall and humble, not doing anything, just being. "You're *real*," my body hums to me, "you're human. It's good enough. Go on."

And what will that look like?

In the form of the moment, it looks like giving sessions and teaching classes from my new office in Salt Lake City. Good will in my family. Paradigm-bridging, sometimes through modeling, sometimes through writing, as in the forthcoming book on *The Body's Map of Consciousness.* New models of higher dimensions, through which we will continue to explore states of consciousness where healing is possible as soon as the plasticity of perception is recognized.

As for its future forms—who can tell?

In the IA world, you build up your willingness to accept the invitation to change. Sometimes you despair because most of the planet won't accept the here-and-now of such extradimensionality, such voluntary limitlessness. You know you can do miracles with it; given time to practice, you know there would be no activity unaltered by its implications—not running marathons, not driving cars, not eating or breathing or teaching English or making love. Perhaps especially not interaction with other humans—that's the most susceptible, you might hope, to creation of a new thing: community, global cooperation, compassion. Conviction drives you to a height of sensitivity, a rawness that almost shuts you down—

"When you first start out
you have more choices
than you do later
—a single dot  . can end up an arc (
or a line -
or even a geometric shape *
—but by the time you're quite a bit further down the road
there's only one stroke you can make
and still make the shape
your work is intended to have.
That there is one final stroke
does NOT mean there is only one way to make it.
Nevertheless, if you don't complete it:
violation of law, void contract.
Everything you've done up to now doesn't count."


"The more clarity
and awareness
you have, the more dire
the consequences of not using them."


"Assess your progress up to now.
Where have you come? What have you accomplished?
Is it better served by gathering support for it?
by integrating a lot to it?
or by giving it wings?"

until you realize it would be harder to go back. All you can do is go forward to increase the range and volume of this expandedness.

So I choose, without knowing the consequences, and relax into "what I really want," and for a nanosecond—no more than that—I have a glimpse of it—like a choice point during a table session, a satellite fly-by of the polarity-neutral null point, the fulcrum from which anything is possible. It's *that* I want—*that* at the base of any decision. The more I allow myself choice—the more tools I have for dissolving at will what stops me—the more the universe opens up. The ultimate tool is my physical structure, *including and especially its limits,* which are not a measure of evil but a source of infinite data through which to explore everything as I become curious and connected enough—energy and consciousness, all perceptions, responsibility and relationship, community and service and Source—and through which to evolve into everything I came here to be.

*"Please feel free to dangle in the wind*
*till you realize*
*you're growing wings."*

To order further copies of this book or *The Body's Map of Consciousness Volume I Physical, Emotional, and Mental Bodies* (due late fall 1999), photocopy the form below and mail it with check or money order to:

NoneTooSoon Publishing          Touchstone
893 S. McClelland          **or**          429 E. Cotati Ave
Salt Lake City UT 84102          Cotati CA 94931
801-363-1747          707-795-4399

Please send _____copies of
*Ask Anything and Your Body Will Answer*

and _____ copies of *The Body's Map of Consciousness I* (late fall '99)

to

(Name)
(Address)
(City, State, Zip)
(Phone/email)

Enclosed is a check or money order for _____($12.95 per copy) plus shipping and handling ($4 for up to 5 books; call for discount and shipping rates over that number).